Smoothies!

STELLA MURPHY

This edition published by Barnes and Noble by arrangement
with New Holland Publishers (UK) Ltd

2005 Barnes and Noble

M 10 9 8 7 6 5 4 3 2 1

ISBN 0-7607-7308-4
Library of Congress Cataloging in Publication data available

To Lucy Murphy – thanks for all the help with the text
and tasting!

SENIOR EDITOR: Clare Hubbard
EDITOR: Anna Bennett
DESIGN CONCEPT: Christelle Marais
DESIGNER: Ian Sandom
PHOTOGRAPHY: Stuart West
PHOTOGRAPH PAGE 12: Shona Wood
FOOD STYLING: Stella Murphy
PRODUCTION: Hazel Kirkman
EDITORIAL DIRECTION: Rosemary Wilkinson

Reproduction by Pica Digital PTE Ltd, Singapore
Printed and bound by Tien Wah Press, Malaysia

SMOOTHIES!

BARNES & NOBLE
NEW YORK

CONTENTS

Smooth talking 8
Equipment blitz 12
Juicy ingredients 18
Top tips 24
The look 26
Important notes 28

Just juice 30
Fruit and vegetable smoothies 62
Real smooth blends 96
Supercharged 136
Indulge 162

Index 190
Acknowledgments 192

SMOOTH

TALKING

What is a smoothie? Is it a drink that is just made from fruit? Or from fruit and vegetables? Is it fruit blended with yogurt, ice cream, or sorbet? The consensus amongst purists is that a smoothie is produced by blending the fruit, the whole fruit, and nothing but the fruit. The difference between a smoothie and a juice is that in a smoothie the whole fruit is used, whereas a juice is the extracted juice only.

Well, I've never been one for sticking to the rules, so in this book I've given you a little bit of everything—pure juices, 100-percent fruit and vegetable smoothies, fruit and vegetable blends combined with dairy and nondairy foods, smoothies with natural additions to enhance well-being, and a wickedly indulgent chapter of luscious concoctions using sorbet and ice cream. Whatever you want to call them, the most important thing is the flavor—and they all taste absolutely delicious.

WHY MAKE YOUR OWN?

There has been an explosion recently in the number of different juice and smoothie products on the market—all attractively packaged for

us to pick up off the shelf and drink on the move. They are an easy and convenient way for us to consume part of our quota of fruit and vegetables required daily, when we are all so busy rushing around with not a moment to spare. Why bother with all that peeling and chopping and having to wash the blender when there are literally hundreds of readymade drinks to choose from? There are a number of very good answers to that question, the most important one being that when you make your own drink you know exactly what's in it. Many of the readymade products contain added sugar, preservatives, and artificial colors, and they can be expensive. Fresh, homemade juices and smoothies provide an immediate and more potent source of nutrients than readymade products that have a shelf-life of a few days. They are also much cheaper. The other great advantage of making your own drinks is that you can mix and match a variety of ingredients to suit your individual taste and dietary requirements.

THE BENEFITS

As well as improving your general well-being, juices and smoothies made purely from fruits and vegetables can have some marked health benefits. The following list sums up just some of the benefits associated

with drinking juices and smoothies on a regular basis:

- Clearer skin.
- Higher energy levels.
- Relief from some ailments, such as colds, stress, insomnia, and depression.
- Some food combinations are also claimed to help prevent certain illnesses, such as cancer. This does not mean that you should drink eight glasses of freshly made fruit or vegetable juices/smoothies a day, however. These drinks should be part of a balanced diet. If you are new to fresh juices and smoothies start with no more than two servings a day and, once you are more accustomed to them, never exceed four servings. Vary the fruits and vegetables that you use in order to obtain a broad range of nutrients.

While the pure juices and smoothies in this book are a healthy option, some of the smoothies contain whole Greek yogurt, cream, and ice cream. Although these drinks are delicious, they are definitely for those times when you want to spoil yourself and should not form a regular part of your daily food intake!

EQUIPMENT BLITZ

THE HEAVY MACHINERY

Before you begin making the juices and smoothies in this book you will need to check that you have the right equipment—basically a juicer and a blender. Many different types are available but try not to skimp. The more expensive appliances will last longer than their cheaper counterparts and will produce noticeably better results, which in turn will yield greater health benefits. Always follow the manufacturer's instructions and ensure that each piece of equipment is cleaned after use. If you don't, you will regret it—there is nothing worse than dried-on fruit pulp.

Centrifugal juicers

These are the least expensive type of electrical juicers. The fruit and vegetables are ground and then spun. The juice comes out and the pulp dispenses into a separate container. They come in a variety of designs and are perfect for those who are only going to use a juicer occasionally. Centrifugal juicers are not recommended for those who want to drink a high-quality juice as part of their daily routine, however. The end product tends to be thick, cloudy, and contains a lot of pulp. An added disadvantage is that enzymes can be destroyed in the juicing process.

Masticating juicers

These are more high-tech than centrifugal juicers and consequently more expensive. They work in a slightly different way to the centrifugal juicers: for example, instead of shredding the ingredients, they chop them finely then force the pulp through a mesh to separate the juice. They also run at a slower speed, which causes less friction and therefore creates less heat. This means the drink will have a fresher taste and be of a higher quality. Masticating juicers produce more juice than

centrifugal ones, and the juices are clearer and more nutritious as they retain more live enzymes, fiber, vitamins, and trace minerals. Some of the more expensive models come with additional attachments that enable you to make baby foods, nut butter, ice creams, sorbets, and sauces.

Citrus juicers

There are three main types:

Electronically operated—this extracts the juice into a container.

Manually-operated hydraulic presser—this squeezes the juice into a container.

Hand-operated squeezer—this uses a ridge to hold back the seeds and a base to retain the juice. This means that the juice and seeds are kept separate.

Opposite left A good-quality blender is indispensable.
Opposite right A smoothie maker is a fun kitchen gadget to have.

Although they are perfect for all citrus fruits, you may still prefer to use a juicer or blender in order to retain the fiber and pulp of the fruit.

Blenders

Drinks made in a blender are more nutritious than those made in a juicer because they retain the fiber from the fruit and vegetables. For best results choose soft fruits, such as berries, bananas, and peaches, and add a liquid ingredient such as water, milk, or fruit juice. It is best to buy quite a high-powered machine because this will produce a smoother drink. Some blenders can cope with ice but others can't, so you should always check the manufacturer's instructions first or you risk damaging the blade.

Smoothie makers

These machines are specifically designed to make smoothies. They blend and foam the ingredients into a smooth, frothy drink. Most machines can cope with the addition of frozen fruits, ice cream, and ice cubes. (always check manufacturer's instructions). They are usually fitted with a dispenser tap through which you can pour the drink, rather than having to remove the jug. I prefer to use a blender because they are more durable if you are making smoothies on a regular basis.

Other useful equipment

You may find it helpful to have the following when making your juices and smoothies:

Sharp knives — essential for preparing fruit and vegtables.

Plastic spatula — ideal for scraping thick blends out of your blender.

Chopping boards — useful when preparing fruit and vegetables.

Vegetable scrubbing brush — this can be used to remove dirt from vegetables as an alternative to peeling. This means that the nutrients and minerals found in and just under the skin can be retained.

Cherry pitter — takes the hard work out of pitting cherries.

Apple corer — this little gadget makes coring apples and pears a much easier and quicker job than doing it with a knife.

Zesters — these are useful for grating the rinds of citrus fruits

to add to recipes and also to create swirls of rind to use as garnishes.

Cannelle knife — this works in a similar way to a zester, but you get much longer ribbons of zest.

Ice cream scoops — these will help you scoop ice cream, frozen yogurts, and sorbets easily. A tip: dip the ice cream scoop into hot water between each scoop in order to stop the ice cream from sticking.

Measuring jugs and spoons — it is useful to keep a selection of these handy.

Ice-crushing machine – this isn't an essential piece of equipment, since many blenders and smoothie makers will do the job. To crush ice by hand lay a clean cloth on a work counter. Spread ice cubes over one half of the cloth and fold the other half over to cover the ice. Use a heavy implement, such as a mallet, to crush the ice, striking firmly. Unfold the cloth and, with a spoon, scrape the crushed ice lightly away from the cloth. Transfer the crushed ice to a jug or glasses.

Vegetable peeler — this enables you to peel vegetables neatly and swiftly, and is much easier than using a knife.

Scales — properly calibrated scales will ensure you use exactly the correct quantity stipulated in the recipe.

Strainer — this is useful for thinning down liquids and removing the seeds from fruit.

Glass or plastic jars with lids — used for storing and chilling juices in the refrigerator for short periods of time.

Lemon squeezer — keep one of these in the cupboard. They are invaluable for producing almost instant citrus juice to add to recipes.

Opposite left *Sharp knives are essential for preparing fruits and vegetables.*

Opposite right *Electronic scales are the most efficient.*

JUICY
INGREDIENTS

The drink that comes out of your juicer or blender will only be as good as the ingredients that you put in. Try to shop with this in mind. If you're making a healthy juice it makes sense to avoid fresh produce that is likely to have been sprayed with pesticides. If you're making an indulgent smoothie don't use poor-quality yogurt or ice cream that's going to be lacking in that all-important creamy taste and texture. If you're going to take the time to make your own drinks, make them as good-quality as they possibly can be.

FRUIT AND VEGETABLES

The fruit and vegetables you use in your juices and smoothies will have a massive impact on the flavor of your drink and its quality. Try to remember these few simple points when you are buying your ingredients:

• Buy seasonal fruit and vegetables whenever possible.

• The riper the fruit is, the sweeter the resulting flavor. It will also give a better yield.

• Ensure that the produce is unblemished.

- Buy organic produce where possible as it is pesticide-free, purer, and better for you. If you are not using organic ingredients you can peel the fruits and vegetables prior to using them in a recipe if you prefer.

- For convenience (and if fresh produce is unavailable), dried, canned, frozen, or bottled fruit and vegetables can be used. Opt for the best quality you can find.

- When soft fruit is in season, large quantities can be purchased and frozen for use later.

Preparation

There are a few simple things that you need to bear in mind before using the fruit and vegetables:

- All fruit, vegetables, and herbs should be washed before use.

- The fruits and vegetables that you use should not only be as fresh as possible, but also visually perfect. This means they should be free from all blemishes and bruises and not overripe.

- Fruits with inedible skins, such as bananas and mangoes, should be peeled before use.

Hard fruits — you will need to use a juicer for hard fruits, such as apples and pears. Cut them into quarters and remove the stems.

Soft and pitted fruits – these can be juiced using a blender or food processor.

- Make sure you destem berries where needed.

- Remove pits before using.

Dried fruits — these need to be soaked for a few hours in hot water to rehydrate them prior to use.

Root and tuber vegetables — these must be juiced using a centrifugal or masticating juicer.

Dairy and nondairy produce

The same rules apply—buy the best quality that you can, organic wherever possible.

Lowfat/skim milk — opt for these if you want a healthier drink or are counting the calories. They are calcium-rich but lower in fat and calories than whole milk.

Whole milk — rich and creamy but high in saturated fat.

Cream — for indulgent recipes and treats, a variety of creams may be used e.g. light or heavy. Cream is high in saturated fat.

Creamy fat-free yogurt — fat-free, and low in calories.

Live bio yogurt — this can help improve the digestive system because it contains healthy bacteria. It is rich in calcium, and is often suitable for those who suffer from lactose intolerance.

Greek yogurt — this is much thicker than standard varieties of yogurt but it is extremely high in calories and should therefore only be used for the occasional treat. Lower-fat options are available.

Reduced-fat coconut milk — a good alternative to whole varieties.

Almond milk — a nondairy alternative, low in cholesterol, and with no added sugar. Suitable for vegetarians and rich in mono-unsaturated fats.

Rice milk — this has a thinner consistency to cow's milk and has a very sweet flavor. Rice milk also comes in a variety of flavors, such as chocolate and vanilla.

Soy milk — a nondairy alternative to cow's milk and gluten-free.

Oat milk — an alternative to cow's milk, with a rich, creamy, and smooth taste.

Buttermilk — high in calcium, low in fat, and an aid to digestion.

Ice cream — virtually every flavor imaginable is now available. There are also many lowfat, low-sugar, and similarly health-conscious varieties on the market too. Buy the best quality ice cream that you can afford.

Tofu — also known as soy beancurd. Tofu comes in three different textures—firm, medium-firm, and silken. Because tofu is naturally bland, it will affect the texture, rather than the taste, of the drink. Silken tofu is the best variety to use when blending because of its creamy, thick texture.

Natural additions

I'm sure that you will be familiar with most of the ingredients used in this book, but there may be a few, such as the natural additions used in the Super-charged chapter (see pages

136–161) that may be new to you. **The important thing to note about these additions is that they must be used according to the manufacturer's instructions and you should check that the product is suitable for you.**

Bee pollen — considered to be one of nature's most complete foods, bee pollen contains all 22 amino acids, minerals, vitamins, and enzymes. It's a great energy booster, a source of protein, and can help reduce the effects of stress.

Echinacea — stimulates the immune system and the lymphatic system. Echinacea comes in capsule, extract, and tea forms.

Flaxseed oil — useful for vegetarians and those who don't eat fish. Rich in omega-3 essential fatty acid, alpha linolenic, and can be converted in the body to the fatty acids EPA and DHA, which are those present in fish. Said to reduce the risk of heart disease and other ailments. Flaxseeds are available in ground form and as oil.

Spirulina — a microscopic algae in the shape of a coil. Now being called a "superfood". Contains the highest concentration of nutrients known in any one food, plant, grain, or herb. Available to buy in powder and capsule form.

Wheat germ — an excellent source of B vitamins, vitamin E, folic acid, iron, magnesium, and potassium. Available in flaked form or as an extracted oil.

Wheatgrass — the grains of wheat that have sprouted until they become young grass. It is said to be cleansing and boosting to the immune system—an all-round tonic.

TOP TIPS

- Make sure that your smoothies are cold when served.
- Juices and smoothies are made for drinking immediately. Their nutritional value decreases the longer they are exposed to air, and some fruit and vegetable juices tend to separate quickly. It is therefore not advisable to store them for more than 1 day.
- If your smoothie is too thick, water it down with still mineral water or another fruit juice (apple is a good mixer); if it is too thin add yogurt for extra body.
- Drinks that are too tart can be sweetened with a little honey.
- Experiment with different fruits and vegetables to make your own unique drinks. Make sure you don't use too many ingredients in any one recipe, however, because this will overpower the drink and mask individual flavors.
- In general you need to take care when mixing fruit and vegetable juices—some can cause flatulence or bloating. The exceptions to this are carrot and apple, which are very good mixer juices in themselves.
- Freeze puréed fruit in ice cube trays and use the fruit ice cubes to add additional flavor to your drinks.
- Frozen fruits work extremely well in smoothies.

THE LOOK

Presentation probably isn't going to be your top priority if you're drinking your smoothie first thing in the morning before rushing off to work, but if you have friends staying for the weekend or are hosting a family brunch party, it's fun to serve up something that looks special.

CLASS IN A GLASS

There is a huge array of glassware available, in every color, size, and shape imaginable. Plastic picnic glasses have also become very stylish—perfect if you're planning an alfresco dining experience. Even fun paper cups, with spotted and striped designs, can look great in the right context. Do think carefully about which glass your drink will look best in, and try to stick to clear glass wherever possible. Many of the drinks featured in this book won't look particularly great if poured into colored glasses: the combination of the color of the glass and the color of the juice can sometimes produce a murky-looking result.

STIR IT UP

Cocktail swizzle sticks, straws, little umbrellas, and long-handled spoons all make good accessories for smoothies. They are fun additions if you're serving the drinks at a party or picnic.

THE FINISHING TOUCH

The kind of garnish that you choose will obviously depend on what type of drink you're having and the ingredients it contains, and it will also to some extent be dictated by the context in which you are drinking or serving it. Obviously, it would not be sensible to top a healthy pure fruit smoothie with crushed chocolate cookies. Similarly, you wouldn't finish off a luxurious ice cream smoothie with a sprinkling of wheat germ. Here are just a few ideas—slices of fruit, citrus curls, herb sprigs, nuts, and berries for the healthy option and crushed cookies, grated chocolate, flavored sauces or a scoop of ice cream for moments of indulgence.

IMPORTANT NOTES

- Each recipe makes one drink or serving.
- Those new to drinking pure fruit and vegetable juices and smoothies should drink no more than two servings a day. Four servings a day is the maximum for a more seasoned drinker. For maximum nutrient intake, vary the fruits and vegetables you use.
- You must always dilute 100-percent pure fruit and vegetable juices and smoothies that are to be served to children. Still mineral water is best for this, but you could use lemonade, sparkling water, soda, or milk, as appropriate.
- If using herbal remedies or supplements always read the information supplied by the manufacturer to check that the product is suitable for you. If in doubt, consult a medical practitioner. Omitting the herbal supplements will not affect the flavor or overall quality of the drink.
- Consult your doctor before taking any supplements at all if you are pregnant, breastfeeding, elderly, or taking any prescribed medication.
- Beets should only ever be used in small quantities, and should never be drunk as a juice on their own because they can cause stomach upsets and nausea.

- You should always consult your doctor before drinking large quantities of grapefruit juice if you are taking prescribed medication.
- Do not use the leaves of rhubarb because they are poisonous. You should always cook rhubarb before eating it or adding it to a recipe because of the high levels of oxalic acid it contains.

JUST JUICE

Simple, hot, and cold combinations of pressed, pure fruit and vegetable juices.

Cherry Delight

A light and refreshing drink.

1 apple, quartered and cored
1 pear, quartered and cored
1/3 cup/50g cherries, stalks removed and pitted
Ice cubes to serve
Fresh mint sprig to garnish

Juice the apple, pear, and cherries together. Pour into a glass over ice. Garnish with a mint sprig.

Summer
Breeze

A cooling summer drink.

1 orange, peel removed and quartered
1¼ cups/200g black grapes, stalks removed
1 pear, quartered and cored
Ice cubes to serve
Twist of lime to garnish

Juice the orange, grapes, and pear together. Pour into a glass over ice. Garnish with a twist of lime.

Summer Sunset

A colorful summer aperitif.

1 pomegranate, cut in half and seeds
scooped out

1 orange, peeled and quartered

Crushed ice to serve

2 tsp orange flower water

Juice the fruits separately.
Pour the pomegranate juice into the
glass first over crushed ice.
Top with the orange juice and stir in
the orange flower water.

Red Velvet

A ruby-red drink with a
delicate aroma.

1 pomegranate, cut in half and seeds
scooped out

2/3 cup/175g raspberries

1 tsp rose water

Juice the fruits and stir
in the rose water.
Serve in a shot glass.

Ruby Reviver

A sharp, reviving drink.

1 blood orange, peeled and quartered

1 lime, peeled and halved

1 passionfruit, cut in half and the pulp scooped out

Ice—cubes or crushed to serve

Juice the orange and lime together.
Stir the passionfruit
pulp into the juice.
Pour into a glass over ice.

In the Pink

A tart-tasting cool-me-down.

1 pink grapefruit, peeled and quartered
3/4 cup/75g cranberries, fresh or frozen
1 apple, quartered and cored
Ice—cubes or crushed to serve

Juice together the grapefruit and cranberries, then add the apple and blend together. Pour into a glass over ice and serve chilled.

Grape Surprise

Thirst-quenching and perfect for a hot day.

1¼ cups/200g red grapes, stalks removed
1¼ cups/200g white grapes, stalks removed
1 apple, quartered and cored
6 fresh mint leaves (apple mint is nice)
Ice—cubes or crushed to serve

Juice together the grapes and apple. Stir in the mint leaves. Pour into a glass over ice. For a long, cool drink dilute with sparkling mineral water.

Christmas Cracker

A spiced Christmas drink.

1¼ cups/275g black currants, stalks removed
2 blood oranges, peeled and quartered
½-in/1-cm piece ginger, peeled
Crushed ice to serve
Extra black currants to garnish

Juice the black currants, oranges, and ginger together. Pour into a glass over crushed ice. Garnish.

Winter Warmer

Warm and spicy—ideal for a cosy winter's night.

2 pears, quartered and cored
1 apple, quartered and cored
2 whole star anise

Juice the fruit together and pour into a saucepan. Add the star anise. Bring slowly to a boil and allow to infuse. Pour into a glass and serve warm.

Cucumber Cooler

Cooling, with a hint of aniseed.

7oz/200g cucumber

4oz/110g fennel bulb, outer part removed,
cut into chunks

5oz/150g tender asparagus, trimmed

Ice cubes to serve

1 sprig fennel frond to garnish

Juice the cucumber, fennel, and
asparagus together. Pour into a glass over
ice. Garnish.

Carrot Crazy

A **vibrant** and **creamy** health _juice._

6oz/175g carrots, trimmed
2 celery stalks, trimmed
1 apple, quartered and cored
Crushed ice to serve

Juice the **carrots, celery,** and **apple** together. **Pour** into a glass over **crushed ice**.

Wonder Whirl

A rich juice with a peppery tang.

3/4oz/20g wheatgrass, rinsed and chopped
1 small garlic clove, peeled
2 celery stalks, trimmed
3oz/75g watercress
Ice cubes to serve
Extra blades of wheatgrass to garnish

Juice the wheatgrass, garlic,
and celery together, then juice
the watercress a little at a time.
Blend the two mixtures together.
Pour into a glass over ice and garnish
with wheatgrass.

Beet Cleanser

A *flame-red*, hot, and *fiery* juice.

2oz/50g beetroot
½-in/1-cm piece ginger, peeled
1 apple, quartered and cored
6oz/175g carrots, trimmed
Fresh parsley to garnish

Juice all of the **ingredients** together.
Pour into a glass and **serve chilled**,
garnished with **parsley**.

Thai Treat

A spicy juice bursting with flavor.

8oz/225g cucumber
8oz/225g carrots, trimmed
½ small chile, deseeded
2-in/5-cm piece lemongrass
1 Tbsp fresh cilantro, chopped
Crushed ice to serve
1 lemon slice to serve

Juice the cucumber, carrots, chile and lemongrass together. Stir in the cilantro. Pour into a glass over ice and serve with a lemon slice.

Fennel and Orange Fantasy

A delicate juice with a subtle taste.

6oz/175g fennel bulb, outer part removed,
cut into chunks
1 orange, peeled and quartered
½oz/10g fresh dill
1 orange slice, quartered to garnish

Juice the fennel, then add
the orange and dill and juice.
Place in a saucepan and heat slowly.
Pour into a glass and serve warm. Garnish
with orange slice.

FRUIT AND VEGETABLE SMOOTHIES

Delicious combinations of blended fruits and vegetables.
Easy to make, healthy, and delicious.

Cherry Charmer

Creamy and delicate.

4 ice cubes
2/3 cup/110g cherries, stalks removed and pitted
3/4 cup/150g strawberries, hulled
1 pear, peeled, quartered, and cored
Fresh mint leaves and strawberries to garnish

Put the ice cubes into the blender and whizz. Add the rest of the ingredients and blend until smooth. Pour into a glass and garnish with mint and strawberries.

Cherry Rose

Palate-cleansing and refreshing.

11oz/300g watermelon, peeled (and seeded
if preferred)
2/3 cup/110g cherries, stalks and pits removed
1/2 cup/100ml apple juice
Crushed ice to serve
Extra watermelon, chopped, to garnish

Put the watermelon into the blender
and blend until seeds are broken up.
Add the cherries and apple juice.
Blend until smooth. Pour into a glass
over crushed ice and garnish
with chopped watermelon.

Berry Dazzler

Rich, velvety, and smooth.

4 ice cubes
1¼ cups/150g cranberries
⅔ cup/150g blueberries
½ cup/100ml pear juice
Extra cranberries and blueberries to garnish

Place the ice cubes in the blender and whizz. Add the rest of the ingredients and blend until smooth. Pour into a glass and serve chilled, garnished with extra cranberries and blueberries.

Red Silk

Decadent and delicious.

½ cup/75g strawberries,
hulled and chopped

¼ cup/75g raspberries

¼ cup/75g blackberries

⅔ cup/150ml apple juice

Crushed ice to serve

Extra raspberries and blackberries to garnish

Place all of the fruits and juice in the
blender and blend until smooth.
Pour into a glass over ice and garnish
with raspberries and blackberries.

Sunny Morning

Orange-speckled with a creamy, flowery taste.

3 ice cubes
1 pear, peeled, halved, cored, and chopped
3 apricots, halved, pitted, and chopped
1 nectarine, halved, pitted, and chopped
½ cup/100ml pear juice
Extra sliced apricot and nectarine to garnish

Place the ice cubes in the blender and whizz, then add the rest of the ingredients and blend until smooth. Pour into a glass and garnish with sliced apricot and nectarine.

Pineapple Pleasure

Creamy and fresh.

4 ice cubes

1 pear, peeled, quartered, and cored

1/4 medium-size pineapple, peeled, core and eyes removed, and flesh cut into chunks

8 large fresh mint leaves, plus extra to garnish

Place the ice cubes in the blender and whizz, then add the rest of the ingredients and blend until smooth. Pour into a glass and garnish with mint.

Watermelon Wonder

Clean and cooling.

1lb/450g watermelon, peeled, seeded if preferred, and cut into chunks

1 lime, peeled and halved

1 sprig fresh rosemary, needles only

Ice cubes to serve

1 chunk watermelon and extra fresh rosemary to garnish

Place the watermelon, lime, and rosemary in the blender and blend until smooth. Pour into a glass over ice and garnish.

Melon Magic

Fragrant and fresh.

12oz/350g honeydew melon, peeled,
seeded, and cut into chunks
2 kiwifruits, peeled and quartered
4 lychees, peeled and stoned
Extra kiwifruit to garnish

Place all of the ingredients in the blender
and blend until smooth.
Pour into a glass and serve chilled,
garnished with kiwifruit.

Strawberry Melon Surprise

Thick, creamy, and irresistible.

12oz/350g Cantaloupe melon, peeled,
seeded and cut into chunks

1 cup/225g strawberries, hulled

1 tsp vanilla extract

Ice cubes to serve

Strawberry slices to garnish

Place the melon, strawberries,
and vanilla extract in the blender
and blend until smooth. Pour into a
glass over ice and garnish.

Breakfast
Bracer

The perfect morning pick-me-up.

1 pink grapefruit, peeled, seeded
and cut into chunks

1 mango, halved either side of the pit, the flesh
scooped out and cut away from the pit

1 banana, peeled and cut into chunks

Ice cubes to serve

Place the grapefruit, mango, and banana in the blender and blend until smooth. Pour into a glass over ice.

Tropical Morning

A *fruity* and *fragrant* breakfast choice.

1 papaya, peeled, seeded, and cut into chunks

1 passionfruit, cut in half and the pulp scooped out

1/2 cup/100ml fresh orange juice

Ice cubes to serve

Extra papaya chunks and 1 orange slice to garnish

Place the **fruits** and **juice** in the blender and **blend** until **smooth**.
Pour into a glass over **ice** and **garnish** with **papaya chunks** and an **orange slice**.

Guava Glitz

Delicate and exotic.

1 guava, peeled and cut into chunks
Juice of 1/2 lime
1/2 cup/125g strawberries, hulled
2/3 cup/150ml pear juice
Crushed ice to serve
Extra strawberries to garnish

Place the fruits and juice in the blender and blend. Strain to remove the guava seeds. Pour into a glass over ice and garnish with extra strawberries.

Berry Banana Blast

A **thick** and **rich** breakfast smoothie.

²/₃ cup/150g blackberries
²/₃ cup/150g blueberries
1 banana, peeled and cut into chunks
1 cup/225ml apple juice
Ice cubes to serve
Extra blackberries and blueberries
to garnish

Place the **fruits** and **juice** in the blender
and **blend** until smooth. Pour into a glass
over **ice** and **garnish**.

Carrot and Mango Crush

Lunch in a glass.

½ cup/100ml fresh orange juice

1 mango, halved either side of the pit, the flesh scooped out and cut away from the pit

3oz/75g carrots, trimmed and chopped

Crushed ice to serve

Extra mango slice to garnish

Place the orange juice and mango in the blender and blend, then add the carrots and blend until smooth. Pour into a glass over crushed ice and garnish.

Wheatgrass Reviver

Aromatic and zesty.

8 ice cubes
4 kiwifruit, peeled and chopped
1/2oz/10g wheatgrass

Place the ice cubes in the blender and whizz. Add the kiwi then the wheatgrass and blend until smooth.
Pour into a glass.

Scarlet Woman

A summer appetizer.

8oz/250g ripe tomatoes, quartered
8 large fresh basil leaves
3 scallions, trimmed
1 red bell pepper, halved and seeded
Crushed ice to serve
Fresh basil leaves to garnish
Salt and black pepper to taste

Place the **tomatoes, basil leaves, scallions** and **bell pepper** in the blender and blend until **smooth**. Pour into a glass over **ice** and **garnish**. You may like to add **seasoning** to taste.

REAL SMOOTH BLENDS

Fresh fruit and vegetables, juiced and blended with dairy and nondairy foods, to make more substantial combinations.

Yogurt Vanilla Velvet

Smooth and satisfying.

1 cup/200g plain yogurt
1 tsp vanilla extract
1 Tbsp Manuka honey
Juice of 1/2 lemon
1 lemon slice and mint leaf to garnish

Place all of the **ingredients** in the blender and **blend** until **smooth**.
Pour into a glass and serve chilled, garnished with lemon and mint.

Pineapple Lassi

Restorative and cooling.

4 ice cubes

1/4-in/0.5-cm piece ginger, peeled and sliced

1/4 medium-size pineapple, peeled, core and
eyes removed and the flesh cut into chunks

1 cup/200g plain yogurt

1 pineapple wedge to garnish

Place the ice cubes in the blender and whizz. Add the rest of the ingredients and blend until smooth. Pour into a glass and garnish with the pineapple wedge.

Mango Lassi

Delicate, with a hint of spice.

½ cup/100ml still mineral water, chilled
1 mango, halved either side of the pit, the flesh
scooped out and cut away from the pit
½ cup/110g plain yogurt
Pinch of cinnamon
Sliced mango and cinnamon stick to garnish

Place all of the ingredients in the blender
and blend until smooth. Pour into a glass
and garnish with sliced mango and a
cinnamon stick.

Guava Berry Refresher

Fruity and rich.

½ cup/100ml grape juice
1 large guava, peeled and seeded
⅔ cup/150g blueberries
1 pear, peeled, quartered, and cored
½ cup/125g plain yogurt
1 pear slice and extra blueberries to garnish

Place the **grape juice** and **guava** into the blender, then add the rest of the **ingredients** and blend until **smooth**. Pour into a glass and serve chilled. **Garnish.**

Banana Breakfast

Breakfast with a difference.

1 Tbsp brown sugar
1 cup/200ml buttermilk
1 banana, peeled and cut into chunks
Pinch of allspice
Ice cubes to serve

Add the sugar to the buttermilk to dissolve. Then place all of the ingredients in the blender and blend until smooth. Pour into a glass over ice.

Peach Perfection

A good source of **protein,** ideal for **breakfast** or a **light lunch.**

1 peach, halved and pitted
$^2/_3$ cup/150g raspberries
4oz/110g silken tofu
$^1/_2$ cup/100ml nondairy milk
Ice cubes to serve
Extra raspberries to garnish

Place all of the **ingredients** in the blender and **blend** until **smooth.** Pour into a glass over **ice** and **garnish.**

Strawberry Fields

A **sweet** start to the day.

1 cup/225g strawberries, hulled
1 tsp vanilla extract
½ cup/125g strawberry yogurt
½ cup/100ml nondairy milk
Strawberry slices to garnish

Place all of the **ingredients** in the blender and **blend** until **smooth**. Pour into a glass and serve **chilled**, **garnished** with **strawberry slices**.

Berry Bonanza

Deep lilac and pleasantly smooth.

½ cup/100ml pure apple juice
½ cup/125g vanilla yogurt
¼ cup/50g blackberries
¼ cup/50g blueberries
Ice cubes to serve
Extra blackberries and blueberries to garnish

Place the apple juice and yogurt into the blender then add the berries and blend until smooth. Pour into a glass over ice and garnish.

Cranberry Craving

Tangy, smooth, and colorful.

⅔ cup/150ml fresh orange juice
½ cup/125g plain yogurt
1 cup/110g cranberries
⅔ cup/150g raspberries
Ice cubes to serve
Fresh mint leaves to garnish

Place the orange juice and yogurt into the blender, then add the berries and blend until smooth.
Pour into a glass over ice and garnish.

Almond Blossom

Smooth, sweet, and healthy.

½ cup/100ml nondairy milk
2½ cups/25g almonds, shelled and chopped
⅔ cup/110g cherries, stalks removed and pitted
1 pear, peeled, quartered, and cored
4oz/110g silken tofu
Crushed ice to serve

Pour the milk into the blender first,
then add the almonds, cherries,
pear, and tofu and blend. Pour into a
glass and serve chilled over ice.

Kiwi Kiss

Fragrant and summery.

2 kiwifruit, peeled and quartered
Juice of 1/2 lime
2/3 cup/175g strawberries, hulled
1/2 cup/125g strawberry-flavored soy yogurt
1/2 cup/100ml nondairy milk
Ice cubes to serve
Slice of kiwifruit to garnish

Place the kiwifruit, lime juice,
strawberries, yogurt, and milk in
the blender and blend until smooth.
Pour into a glass over ice
and garnish with a slice of kiwifruit.

Banana Berry Blush

A classic flavor combination.

1 banana, peeled and chopped
2/3 cup/175g strawberries, hulled
1/2 cup/125g creamy yogurt
1/2 cup/100ml milk
Ice cubes to serve
Strawberry slices to garnish

Place the banana, strawberries, yogurt, and milk in the blender and blend until smooth. Pour into a glass over ice and garnish.

Coconut Burst

Creamy and tropical.

4 ice cubes

1/2 medium-size pineapple, core and eyes removed and flesh cut into chunks

1 banana, peeled and chopped

1 apple, peeled, quartered, and cored

2/3 cup/150ml light coconut milk

Fresh mint leaves to garnish

Place the ice cubes into the blender first and whizz. Add the rest of the ingredients and blend until smooth. Pour into a glass and serve chilled, garnished with mint leaves.

Minted Cucumber Lassi

Soothing and refreshing.

¹/₄ cucumber, chopped
¹/₂oz/10g fresh mint leaves
¹/₂ cup/125g plain yogurt
Cucumber sticks and fresh mint leaves
to garnish

Place all of the ingredients in a blender and blend until smooth. Pour into a glass and serve chilled, garnished with a stick of cucumber and mint leaves.

Carrot Avocado Cleanser

Healthy and pure.

8oz/250g carrots, trimmed
1/2 avocado, peeled, pitted, and cut into chunks
1/2 cup/110g bean sprouts
1/2 cup/125g plain yogurt
Ice cubes to serve
Carrot sticks to garnish

Juice the carrots. Put the juice into the blender with the avocado, bean sprouts, and yogurt and blend until smooth. Pour into a glass over ice and garnish.

Virgin Mary

A pick-me-up or pre-lunch drink.

10oz/275g ripe red tomatoes, quartered
½ cup/125g plain yogurt
Dash of Tabasco sauce, to taste
Dash of Worcestershire sauce, to taste
Crushed ice to serve
1 celery stalk, with leaves, to garnish

Place the tomatoes, yogurt, and sauces into the blender and blend until smooth. Pour into a glass over crushed ice and garnish with a celery stalk.

Flamenco Fool

A perfect mid-morning snack.

1 cup/225ml still mineral water, chilled

2 sweet red bell peppers, roasted, quartered, seeded, and skinned

½ cup/125g plain yogurt

¼ cup/50g sun-dried tomatoes, chopped

Salt and pepper, to taste

Ice cubes to serve

Fresh basil leaves to garnish

Place the water in the blender first, then add the bell peppers, yogurt, sun-dried tomatoes, and seasoning. Blend. Pour into a glass over ice and garnish with basil leaves.

Herbal Healer

Savory and clean-tasting.

½ cucumber, chopped
¼oz/5g fresh dill
¼oz/5g fresh parsley
1 green bell pepper, seeded and chopped
4 scallions, trimmed
Salt and pepper, to taste
Ice cubes to serve
Cucumber slices to garnish

Place the cucumber in the blender and whizz, then add the herbs, bell pepper, scallions and seasoning and blend until smooth. Pour into a glass over ice and garnish.

Beet Bliss

A vibrant and flavorful drink.

4½oz/125g cooked beets, cut into chunks
½ cup/125g plain yogurt
1 clove garlic, peeled and chopped
½oz/10g fresh chives, chopped
½ cup/100ml apple juice
Extra fresh chives to garnish

Place all of the ingredients in a blender
and blend until smooth.
Pour into a glass and garnish
with chives.

SUPERCHARGED

Supercharged smoothies—energy givers, stress busters, and vitamin boosters.

Apricot and Date Booster

A healthy, **high-fiber** start to the day.

2/3 cup/150ml apple juice
4 semidried, no-soak apricots, chopped
2 medjool dates, chopped
1 fig, chopped
1/2 cup/125g plain yogurt
1 Tbsp wheat germ
Ice cubes to serve

Put the **apple juice** into the blender first, then add the **apricots, dates, fig, yogurt,** and **wheat germ.** Blend until smooth. Pour into a glass over **ice.**

Easy Energizer

Restorative and energizing.

2/3 cup/150ml milk
1/2 cup/125g live yogurt
1/2 avocado, peeled and pitted
1 banana, peeled and chopped
21/2 cups/5g almonds, shelled and chopped
Ice cubes to serve

Put the milk and yogurt into the blender first, then add the avocado, banana, and almonds and blend. Pour into a glass over ice.

Papaya Passion

A **fresh-tasting** digestif.

½ cup/125g live yogurt
1 papaya, peeled and seeded
¼ medium-size pineapple, core and eyes
removed and flesh cut into chunks
½-in/1.5-cm piece ginger, peeled and chopped
Ice cubes to serve

Put the **yogurt** into the blender first,
then add the **papaya, pineapple,** and
ginger. Blend until **smooth**. Pour into a
glass over **ice**.

Raspberry Shake

A creamy, nutty pick-me-up, rich in omega-3.

²/₃ cup/150g raspberries
¹/₄ cup/25g walnuts, chopped
2 tsp flaxseed oil
¹/₂ cup/100ml soy milk

Place all of the ingredients
in the blender and blend until smooth.
Pour into a glass and serve chilled.

Breakfast Elixir

Breakfast in a glass—irresistibly moreish.

3oz/75g mixed dry fruit e.g. apricot,
apple, pear etc., roughly chopped
½ cup/100ml fresh orange juice
½ cup/100ml oat milk
1 banana, peeled and chopped
Toasted oatmeal and a wedge of orange
to garnish

Put the dry fruit in a dish and cover
with hot water. Soak for a few hours. Put the
orange juice and oat milk into the
blender first, then add the dry fruit with
the soaking water and the banana.
Blend until smooth. Pour into a glass and serve
chilled. Garnish.

Apricot and Orange Nectar

Refreshing and reviving.

3 apricots, cut in half and pitted
2 oranges, peeled and cut into chunks
2 drops echinacea
Ice cubes to serve

Place the apricots, oranges, and echinacea in the blender and blend. Pour into a glass over ice.

Raspberry Rapture

A sweet, immune-system booster.

½ cup/125g raspberries
1 cup/110g cranberries
½ cup/100ml apple juice
2 drops echinacea
2 tsp bee pollen
Fresh mint leaves to garnish

Place all of the **ingredients** in the blender and blend until **smooth**. Pour into a glass and serve chilled, **garnished** with **mint leaves**.

Black Currant-Orange Blaze

A sharp, vitamin-C rich smoothie.

½ cup/125g black currants, stalks removed
Juice of ½ large lemon
2 oranges, peeled and cut into chunks
Crushed ice to serve
Lemon slice to garnish

Place the black currants, lemon juice, and oranges in the blender and blend. Pour into a glass over crushed ice and garnish with a lemon slice.

Purple Satin

Rich, clean, and bursting with vitamins.

½ cup/125g black currants, stalks removed
⅔ cup/125g cherries, stalks removed and pitted
1 cup/200ml cold rosehip tea
(use 2 tea bags)

Place all of the ingredients in the blender
and blend until smooth.

Pour into a glass.

Pistachio Rice & Milk Shake

Fragrant, nutty, and protein-rich.

1 cup/200ml rice milk
Generous 1/4 cup/40g pistachios, shelled
Generous 1/4 cup/40g almonds, shelled and chopped
Good pinch of cinnamon
1 tsp fructose (fruit sugar)
1 cinnamon stick to garnish

Put the **rice milk** into the blender first,
then add the rest of the **ingredients**
and blend. Pour into a glass and **garnish**
with a **cinnamon stick**.

Greensleeves

Dark and velvety green, this will give you an instant kick.

2 tsp spirulina
1/2 cup/100ml milk
1/2 cup/125g plain yogurt
1 banana, peeled and chopped
1 Tbsp Manuka honey

Put all of the ingredients in the blender and blend until smooth. Pour into a glass and serve chilled.

Chamomile Calm

Pleasantly **perfumed** and *calming*.

1 cup/200ml cold chamomile tea
(use 2 tea bags)
1 papaya, peeled, halved, and seeded
Ice cubes to serve

Put the **chamomile tea** and **papaya**
in the blender and blend until **smooth**.
Pour into a glass over **ice**.

INDULGE

Extra special smoothie recipes made with indulgent ingredients. Some have an added 'chill' factor, perfect for a hot day.

Raspberry and Orange Slush

An **ice-cold reviver** for a scorching day.

1 cup/200ml blood orange juice

Generous ²/₃ cup/200g frozen raspberries (do not defrost)

2 blood oranges, peeled and cut into chunks

Crushed ice to serve

Put the **orange juice** in the blender first, then add the **raspberries** and **oranges** and **blend** until smooth. Pour into a glass over **crushed ice**.

Kiwi and Lemon Sorbet Crush

Cool, fresh, and reviving.

3 kiwifruit, peeled and cut in half
6oz/175g lemon sorbet

Place the ingredients in the blender
and blend until smooth.

Pour into a glass and serve immediately.

Berry Crush

Tangy and vividly colored.

½ cup/100ml fresh orange juice
¾ cup/75g cranberries
5oz/150g raspberry sorbet
Crushed ice to serve
Raspberries and cranberries to garnish

Put the **orange juice** into the blender first, then add the **cranberries** and **sorbet** and blend until **smooth**. Pour into a glass over **crushed ice** and garnish.

Strawberry and Lime Crush

A fresh, clean summer's drink.

1/4 cup/55ml elderflower cordial
1/2 cup/125g strawberries, hulled
5oz/150g lime sorbet
Crushed ice to serve

Put the **elderflower cordial** into the
blender first, then add the rest of the
ingredients and blend until **smooth**.
Pour into a glass over **crushed ice**.

Gooseberry Custard Fool

Totally and simply divine.

1 cup/200ml lowfat milk

8oz/225g gooseberries (pink-tinged dessert gooseberries are sweeter), topped and tailed

1 cup/200ml good-quality readymade vanilla custard

Ice cubes to serve

Extra gooseberries to garnish

Put the milk into the blender first then add the gooseberries and custard and blend until smooth. Pour into a glass over ice and garnish.

Rhubarb Ruse

One glass of this **delicious** smoothie
will not be **enough.**

3oz/75g cooked rhubarb (do not use the leaves
because they are poisonous)

1¹/₂oz/40g preserved ginger, chopped

1 Tbsp ginger syrup

5oz/150g lowfat vanilla ice cream

Ice cubes to serve

Extra cooked rhubarb to garnish

Place the **cooked rhubarb, ginger,
syrup,** and **ice cream** in the blender
and blend until **smooth.** Pour into a
glass over **ice** and **garnish.**

Blueberry Maple Bouquet

A classic flavor combination.

5oz/150g maple-syrup flavored ice cream
Generous 1/2 cup/150g blueberries
2 Tbsp maple syrup
Ice cubes to serve
Extra blueberries to garnish

Put the ice cream into the blender first, then add the blueberries and maple syrup and blend until smooth. Pour into the glass over ice and garnish.

Banana Bandit

An ideal **dessert** drink.

²/₃ cup/150ml lowfat milk
1 banana, peeled, sliced, and frozen
2 Tbsp toffee sauce
Ice cubes to serve

Put the **milk** into the blender first
then add the **frozen banana** and
toffee sauce and blend until **smooth**.
Pour into a glass over **ice**.

Devil's Delight

Children and chocoholics will adore this **wicked** drink.

6oz/175g white chocolate ice cream
2/3 cup/150ml chocolate milk
2 Tbsp chocolate sauce
Ice cubes to serve

Place the ice cream, chocolate milk, and sauce into the blender and blend until smooth. Pour into a glass over ice.

Coconut
Conspiracy

A fabulously luxurious drink.

1 cup/200ml reduced-fat coconut milk
2 Tbsp chocolate sauce
1 banana, peeled and chopped
Ice cubes to serve

Place the coconut milk, chocolate sauce, and banana in the blender and blend until smooth. Pour into a glass over ice.

Coffee Compulsion

An ideal summer breakfast drink.

1 cup/200ml readymade custard
6oz/175g coffee ice cream
1/2 cup/100ml cold espresso coffee
1 Tbsp caramel syrup
Ice cubes to serve
Chocolate coffee beans to garnish

Put the custard, ice cream, coffee, and syrup into the blender and blend. Pour into a glass over ice and garnish.

Apple Pie

Apple pie in a glass.

¼ cup/25g raisins
6oz/175g cooked, cold apple purée
1 cup/200g vanilla iced yogurt
Good pinch of cinnamon
Ice cubes to serve
1 cookie, crumbled to garnish
Cinnamon stick to garnish
Lowfat vanilla ice cream to serve (optional)

Put the raisins in a dish, cover with hot water, and leave for a few hours. Place the raisins and their soaking water, apple purée, yogurt and cinnamon in the blender and blend. Pour into a glass over ice and garnish. Serve with ice cream.

Pretty in Pink

Pink, smooth, and utterly tempting.

Generous ½ cup/150g raspberries
3 Tbsp chilled still mineral water
⅔ cup/150ml heavy cream
5oz/150g champagne and rhubarb ice cream
2oz/50g meringue, broken
Ice cubes to serve
Raspberries and meringue pieces to garnish

Put the **raspberries** and **water** into the blender first then add the **cream, ice cream,** and **meringue** and blend. Pour into a glass over **ice** and **garnish**.

Index

A

almond milk 22
almonds 117, 141
apples: Apple Pie 187
  Beet Bliss 135
  Cherry Delight 33
  Grape Surprise 45
  Winter Warmer 49
apricots: Apricot and
  Date Booster 139
  Apricot and
  Orange Nectar 149
  Sunny Morning 73
asparagus 51
avocadoes 127, 141

B

bananas: Banana
  Bandit 179
  Banana Berry
  Blush 121
  Banana Breakfast
  107
  Berry Banana Blast
  89
  Coconut
  Conspiracy 183
bee pollen 23, 151
Beet Bliss 135
Beet Cleanser 57
bell peppers:
  Flamenco Fool 131
  Herbal Healer 133
  Scarlet Woman 95
Berry Banana Blast 89
Berry Bonanza 113
Berry Crush 169
Berry Dazzler 69
blackberries 71, 89, 113
black currants 47,
  153, 155

blenders 15
blueberries: Berry
  Banana Blast 89
  Berry Bonanza 113
  Berry Dazzler 69
  Blueberry Maple
  Bouquet 177
  Guava Berry
  Refresher 105
Breakfast Bracer 83
Breakfast Elixir 147
buttermilk 22, 107

C

carrots: Beet
  Cleanser 57
  Carrot and Mango
  Crush 91
  Carrot Avocado
  Cleanser 127
  Carrot Crazy 53
  Thai Treat 59
centrifugal juicers
  13–14
Chamomile Calm 161
cherries: Almond
  Blossom 117
  Cherry Charmer 65
  Cherry Delight 33
  Cherry Rose 67
  Purple Satin 155
chocolate 181, 183
Christmas Cracker 47
citrus juicers 15
coconut milk 21, 123,
  183
Coffee Compulsion
  185
cranberries: Berry
  Crush 169
  Berry Dazzler 69
  Cranberry Craving
  115
  In the Pink 43

Raspberry Rapture
  151
cream 21, 189
cucumber: Cucumber
  Cooler 51
  Herbal Healer 133
  Minted Cucumber
  Lassi 125
  Thai Treat 59
custard 173, 185

D

dairy produce 21–2
dates 139
Devil's Delight 181
dry fruit 147

E

Easy Energizer 141
echinacea 23, 149, 151
elderflower cordial
  171
equipment 13–17

F

fennel 51, 61
Flamenco Fool 131
flaxseed oil 23
fruit 19–21

G

garnishes 27
glasses 26
Gooseberry Custard
  Fool 173
grapefruit 43, 83
grapes 35, 45
Greensleeves 159
Guava Berry
  Refresher 105
Guava Glitz 87

H

Herbal Healer 133

I

ice cream 22
  Blueberry Maple
    Bouquet 177
  Coffee Compulsion
    185
  Devil's Delight 181
  Pretty in Pink 189
  Rhubarb Ruse 175
In the Pink 43
ingredients 19–23

J

juicers 13–15

K

kiwifruit: Kiwi and
    Lemon Sorbet
    Crush 167
Kiwi Kiss 119
Melon Magic 79
Wheatgrass Reviver
    93

L

Lassi 101–3, 125
lemon sorbet 167
lime sorbet 171

M

mangoes: Breakfast
    Bracer 83
  Carrot and Mango
    Crush 91
  Mango Lassi 103
maple syrup 177
masticating juicers
    14–15
melon 79, 81
  see also watermelon
milk 21
  Banana Bandit 179
  Banana Berry
    Blush 121

Easy Energizer 141
milk (nondairy) 21–2
  Almond Blossom
    117
  Kiwi Kiss 119
  Peach Perfection
    109
  Strawberry Fields
    111
Minted Cucumber
  Lassi 125

O

oat milk 22, 147
orange: Apricot and
    Orange Nectar 149
  Berry Crush 169
  Black currant
    Orange Blaze 153
  Breakfast Elixir 147
  Carrot and Mango
    Crush 91
  Christmas Cracker
    47
  Cranberry Craving
    115
  Fennel and Orange
    Fantasy 61
  Raspberry and
    Orange Slush 165
  Ruby Reviver 41
  Summer Breeze 35
  Summer Sunset 37

P

papaya: Chamomile
    Calm 161
  Papaya Passion 143
  Tropical Morning
    85
passion fruit 41, 85
Peach Perfection 109
pears: Pineapple
    Pleasure 75

Sunny Morning 73
  Winter Warmer 49
pineapple: Coconut
    Burst 123
  Papaya Passion 143
  Pineapple Lassi 101
  Pineapple Pleasure
    75
Pistachio Rice Milk
  Shake 158
pomegranate 37, 39
Pretty in Pink 189
Purple Satin 155

R

raisins 187
raspberries: Peach
    Perfection 109
  Pretty in Pink 189
  Raspberry and
    Orange Slush 165
  Raspberry Rapture
    151
  Raspberry Shake
    145
  Red Silk 71
  Red Velvet 39
raspberry sorbet 169
Red Silk 71
Red Velvet 39
Rhubarb Ruse 175
rice milk 22, 158
Ruby Reviver 41

S

Scarlet Woman 95
smoothie makers
    15–16
soy milk 22, 145
spirulina 23, 159
strawberries: Banana
    Berry Blush 121
  Cherry Charmer 65
  Guava Glitz 87

191

Kiwi Kiss 119
Red Silk 71
Strawberry and
  Lime Crush 171
Strawberry Fields
  111
Strawberry Melon
  Surprise 81
Summer Breeze 35
Summer Sunset 37
Sunny Morning 73

T
Thai Treat 59
tofu 22, 109, 117
tomatoes 95, 129
Tropical Morning 85

V
vegetables 19–21
Virgin Mary 129

W
walnuts 145
watercress 55
watermelon 67, 77
wheat germ 23
wheatgrass 23, 55, 93
Winter Warmer 49
Wonder Whirl 55

Y
yogurt 21
  Apple Pie 187
  Banana Berry
    Blush 121
  Beet Bliss 135

Berry Bonanza 113
Cranberry Craving
  115
Easy Energizer 141
Flamenco Fool 131
Greensleeves 159
Guava Berry
  Refresher 105
Kiwi Kiss 119
Mango Lassi 103
Minted Cucumber
  Lassi 125
Papaya Passion 143
Pineapple Lassi 101
Strawberry Fields
  111
Virgin Mary 129
Yogurt Vanilla
  Velvet 99

Acknowledgments

The author and publisher would like to thank:

Denby for supplying glasses and tableware for photography.

The Pier for supplying glasses and tableware for photography.

New Classics for supplying the Waring Kitchen Classic Juicer for recipe testing and the blender for photography (see page 12).